LET'S GO MYGRID!

24 VDC   1000 WATTS   32 AMPS

SOLAR   START-UP

By Stephen P. Brodie

CONTENTS

PRACTICAL SOLAR ON A BUDGET

I have gone "mygrid", in a sense. That means I set up a stand-alone array of solar panels in my back yard, not at all attached to the house electrical panel. These solar panels connect into the house on 12 AWG wires, passing through a DC Fast breaker, then into an MPPT Solar Charge Controller, on to a battery bank, then connecting to an Inverter for Vac use wherever I want. Advantages for going "mygrid" are:

1. No connection into the electrical company's grid.
2. Freedom to add more panels, batteries, etc. without concern for a grid tie-in or transfer switch.
3. No installed middle-man system on the roof that offers a contract to maintain, and thus bill me for!

There is satisfaction to DYI (Do It Yourself) and reducing dependence on electrical supply company pricing. A stand-alone setup will have costs up front, but having a 25–30 year use of energy from the sun and being able to upgrade that setup over time, is a good investment.

Once I researched solar power and its components, I began purchasing parts to assemble the system. I purchased most of the parts through Amazon so to utilize their "Prime" option of two days free shipping, and of course to pay over time. I have been very satisfied using Amazon, and continue to as I expand the setup in my yard. Some hardware and grounding cabling came from Home Depot.

Most people can put together a solar setup in their yard; it is not a difficult challenge. You need a small number of components, a little knowledge of connecting them together, and how you want to use this free energy within your home. You learn about YOUR solar by going to what I term "Professor YouTube" and seeking other online information, and then simply having a working system to self-train on. Many others have done this and many more will too. It may be for long-term cost savings, reducing fossil fuels by utilizing the sun's energy, or just for self-reliance measures in case the grid is down. It is a wise investment.

The following pages are meant to move you through system building a small scale, 1000 watt solar array for home use, that you may build upon over time, if desired. I built a 1Kw, 24 Vdc , 32 amp system. The build will be explained, component-by-component, and with graphics and photos throughout.

There is much information and illustrations to work with, but I know some information may have been missed. It does give more than enough to get one started in building and understanding solar, and it is a great prepper survival experience as well as saving future costs in electricity from the grid.

I hope this information is useful and informative.

A general graphic of mygrid:

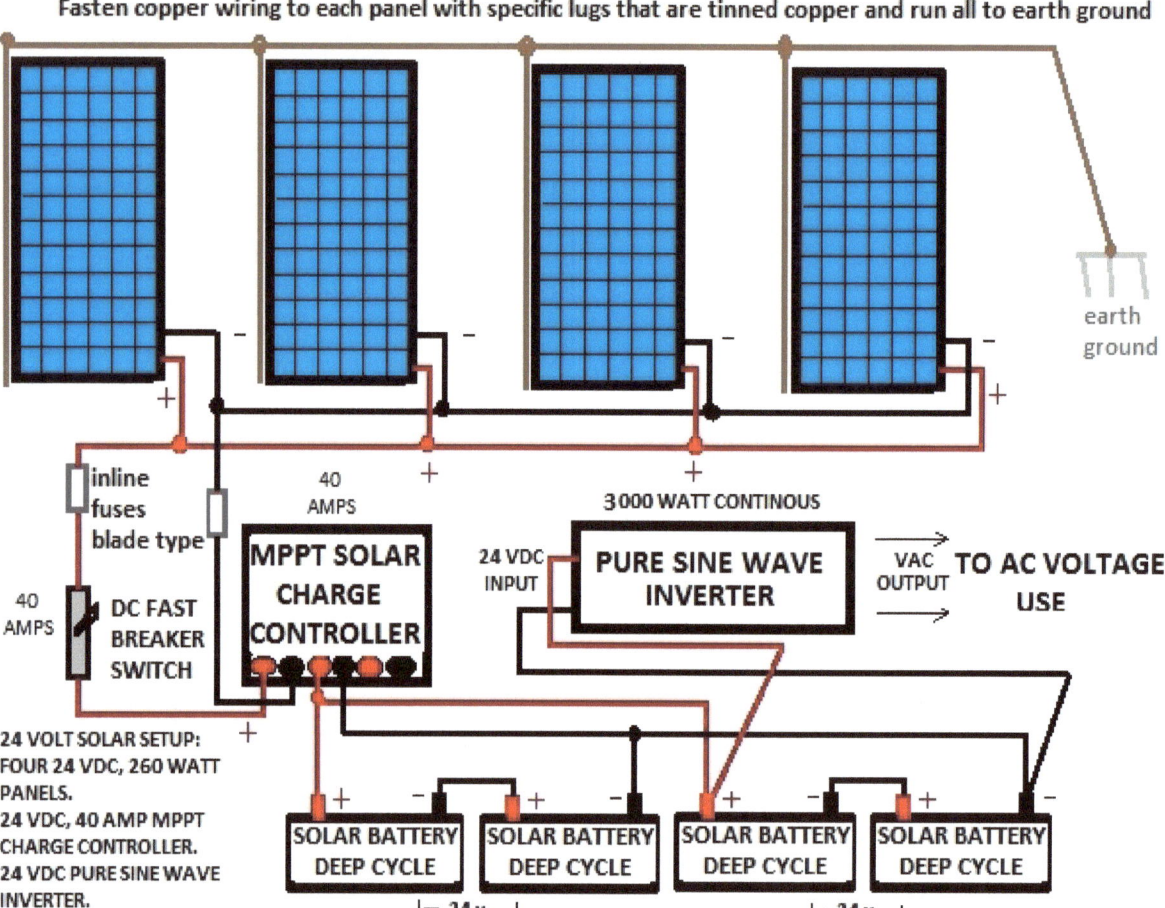

Fasten copper wiring to each panel with specific lugs that are tinned copper and run all to earth ground

earth ground

inline fuses blade type

40 AMPS

3 000 WATT CONTINOUS

MPPT SOLAR CHARGE CONTROLLER

24 VDC INPUT

PURE SINE WAVE INVERTER

VAC OUTPUT   TO AC VOLTAGE USE

40 AMPS

DC FAST BREAKER SWITCH

24 VOLT SOLAR SETUP: FOUR 24 VDC, 260 WATT PANELS.
24 VDC, 40 AMP MPPT CHARGE CONTROLLER.
24 VDC PURE SINE WAVE INVERTER.

SOLAR BATTERY DEEP CYCLE

SOLAR BATTERY DEEP CYCLE

SOLAR BATTERY DEEP CYCLE

SOLAR BATTERY DEEP CYCLE

'— 24 v —'   '— 24 v —'

A combiner box may be installed above, if desired, to have all four panels' positive cables and negative cables joined within one enclosed box. This is a good troubleshooting measure to have all connections where they can be tested with a voltmeter to verify each panel's voltage and amps are as expected. The combiner box may be inserted between the above two blade fuses and the fast breaker and charge controller positive (red) and negative (Black) lines. Please see FIG 3 in the chapter, "Connecting it together" and the "Blocking Diode " graphic in the "TERMINOLOGY" section for additional explanation.

2

ELECTRONS

Every element known to man has electrons. Copper is one of these elements. Most of the wiring of solar equipment uses copper wires to connect solar cells together, run external cables to fuses, combiners, charge controllers, battery banks, meters, inverters, then out to appliances. Copper is also used in equipment grounding and lightning protection.

Without the movement of electrons in these wires and cables, not much happens. Electrons receive energy, called charge, and they carry this charge in these wires into your home appliances to make them work. The light you see in the bulb is due to these charge-carrying electrons dissipating that energy into a tiny filament inside the bulb, thus energizing it – lighting it up.

The following graphic may help to explain electrons:

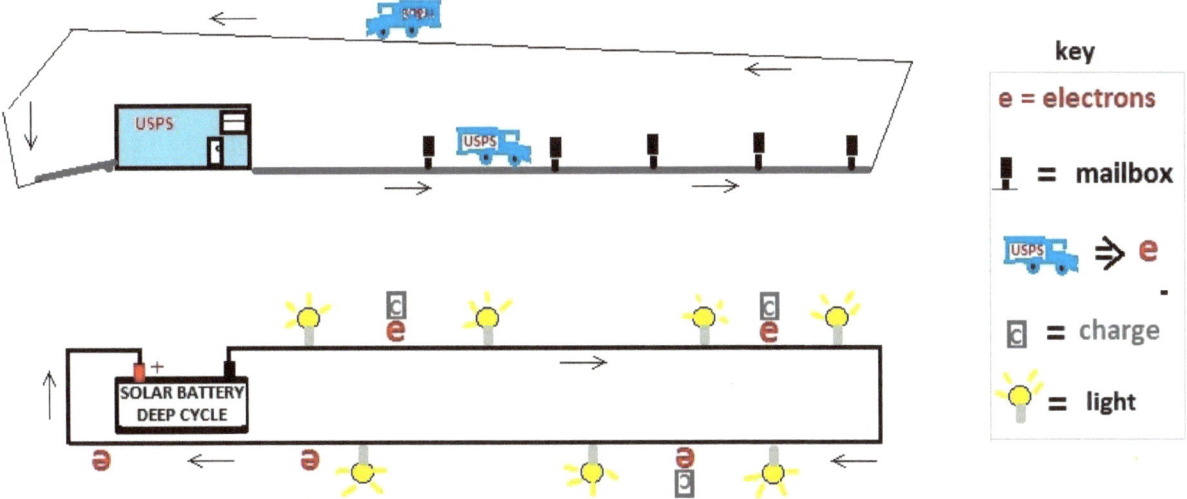

A basic analogy about the charge carrying electron in an electronic circuit:

In this analogy, the postman fills up the truck with mail and delivers it to all mailboxes in town, then brings the empty truck back to the post office to obtain more mail.

The electrons gather up charge in the battery and take it in the wire to every appliance (light bulb fixtures in example) to disperse the charge of energy into the load, or appliance, then returns to the battery source of energy to obtain more energy charge.

As the postman moves on the road, so electrons move on the wire. The wire makes a circuit from source of energy charge back to source, just as the postman makes a circuit from source of mail back to source.

As solar energy, photons, arrive at the solar panels' cells, it adds charge to electrons, and these charge carrying electrons flow out as current into the wiring going to the various solar equipment, then eventually, to either a DC or AC appliance to energize it.

PHOTONS

Photovoltaic effect in a solar panel's single solar cell occurs when the cell is receiving light from the sun. That light is actually energy that comes into contact with millions of electrons within the cell, dislodging them as energy is stored into them. As electrons are charged up, they leave the orbits of their atoms and can flow freely. It's important to note, these charged electrons want to release this energy and return to a static state. If we connect a wire to allow charged electrons to flow through it, they can release the energy into a battery or a direct use such as lighting a bulb, for example. We call these end points a load. The energized electrons will flow through the wire, dissipating their charge into the load, storing that energy into the battery, or lighting up the bulb, and the electrons can return to a static state again. All electronics requires the flow of energized electrons moving through wires or contact paths into loads, and returning to the source. As long as energy is still required by the load, these electrons continue to obtain more charge as they return to source and carry it to the load, over and over.

We could have used a generator whose rotating shaft is being turned by water flowing over a dam or possibly a wind current pushing against large blades turning the shaft. The generator produces energy that excites electrons into a current flow. In the above instance, we are utilizing energy from sunlight.
Sunlight energy is in the form of photons. Photons basically spray out from the sun toward earth, and we try to

retrieve, or harness, as much of their energy as possible into our solar cell(s).

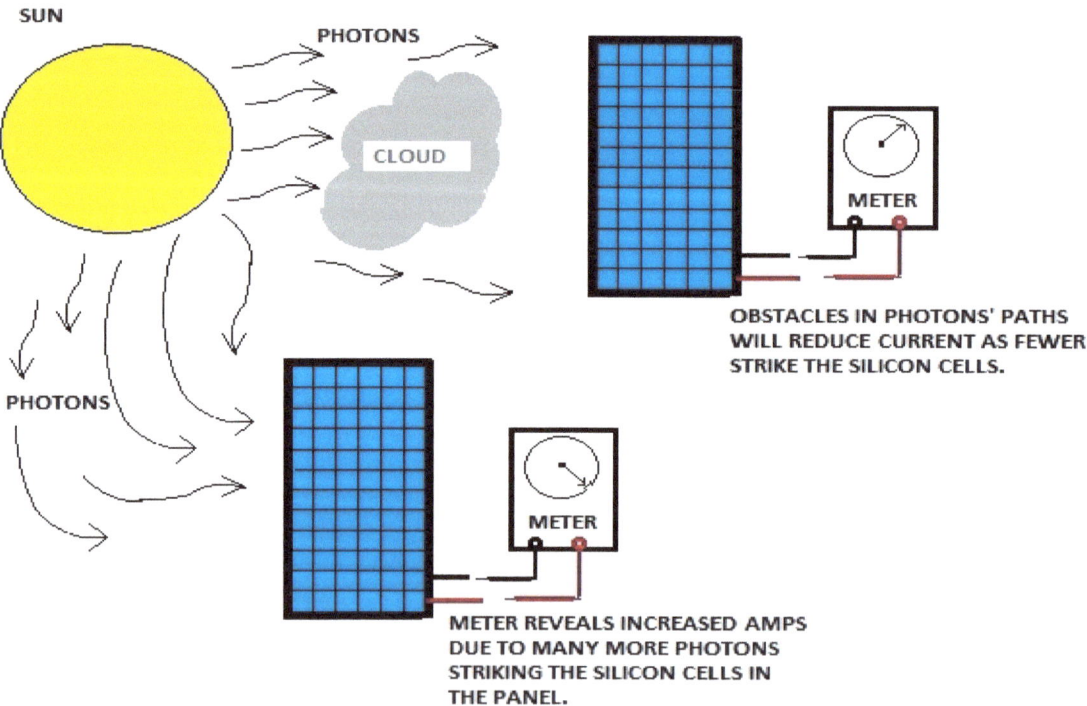

The solar cell is manufactured as a semiconductor, which conducts electricity, electrons, in one direction of flow only. It is fabricated for that purpose. Think of two wafers made of the element silicon sandwiched together. If you know how an atom is modeled, with orbits or rings around a nucleus, having electrons arranged in those rings at specific numbers; the last ring is called a valence ring. Silicon has four electrons in its last or valence ring. If you bring two silicon atoms together, each one's four electrons will bond with the last ring of the other, actually giving us eight electrons. This action within the silicon wafer then makes a strong bond of many silicon atoms making up that wafer. That silicon material is not a semiconductor, yet. To make it such, another element, from the periodic table of elements, must be added into the pure silicon wafers. This process is termed "doping", or adding an impurity to the silicon. If, for example, the element phosphorus, which has five electrons in its outer, valence ring, is added to the silicon, those atoms of phosphorus will have four of their valence ring's five electrons blend or bond with each silicon atom's valence ring's four electrons, causing the remaining 5th electron to become a free electron within the silicon wafer. Now, the second silicon wafer of the two is then doped with the element boron, which has only three electrons in its outer valence ring. When the boron atoms are added to the second silicon wafer, the boron's three electrons will bond with the silicon's outer valence ring's four electrons, giving us only seven electrons, leaving what is termed a "hole" or missing electron space in many silicon/boron bonded atoms in that wafer. The first wafer, having a free electron makes that wafer negative, while the second wafer, missing an electron, is considered positive.

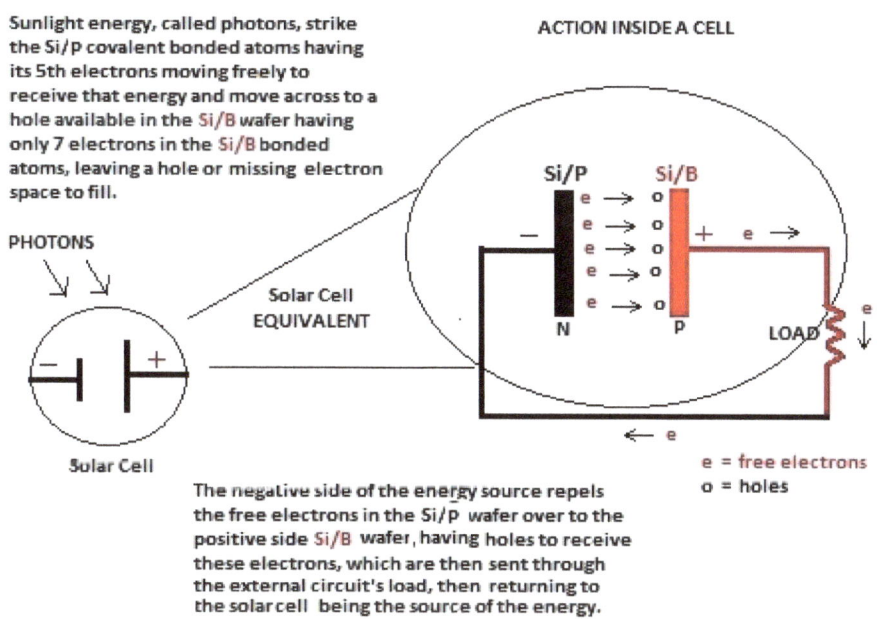

Sunlight energy, called photons, strike the Si/P covalent bonded atoms having its 5th electrons moving freely to receive that energy and move across to a hole available in the Si/B wafer having only 7 electrons in the Si/B bonded atoms, leaving a hole or missing electron space to fill.

ACTION INSIDE A CELL

PHOTONS

Solar Cell EQUIVALENT

Solar Cell

The negative side of the energy source repels the free electrons in the Si/P wafer over to the positive side Si/B wafer, having holes to receive these electrons, which are then sent through the external circuit's load, then returning to the solar cell being the source of the energy.

e = free electrons
o = holes

Si/p is Silicon bonded with Phosphorous, Si/B is Silicon bonded with Boron.

If we bring these two wafers together, and place a source of energy across them, such as a battery, (or a solar panel), having its negative pole connected to the negative wafer, and its positive pole connected to the wafer which is positive, the free electrons will be compelled across to the positive wafer, contacting a hole there. Millions of these transitions across constitute a current flow. This entire process occurs in one direction and makes this material a semiconductor. This is what a solar cell does. Instead of using a battery, it utilizes sunlight energy. If wires are connected to either side of the wafer, negative and positive sides, then energy flowing in those displaced electrons will cause a current to reach a load, such as a battery bank or other type use.

The energy coming from these solar cells is termed VDC, Voltage Direct Current. Most battery operated devices and the batteries, are VDC. If you wanted to go to VAC, Voltage Alternating Current, like that current used in common home appliances, you could send the VDC into an inverter, which converts the VDC to VAC.

After the initial costs involved in setting up a home solar system, you have built a source of free energy, using sunlight! As long as there is sunlight, you have decades of free electricity. And, that is the caveat.

A Solar grid depends on photons. The rainy days and shaded areas bring in little or no light energy. But, it is still worth setting up solar. As money is available, more panels and batteries may be employed to capture and store more energy day-to-day. This definitely effects the electrical bill and still is a great self-reliance measure for when the local grid goes down. It is insurance against the rainy day to have stored energy at the ready. There is no real downside to a solar setup, in my opinion.

BUILDING THE PANEL

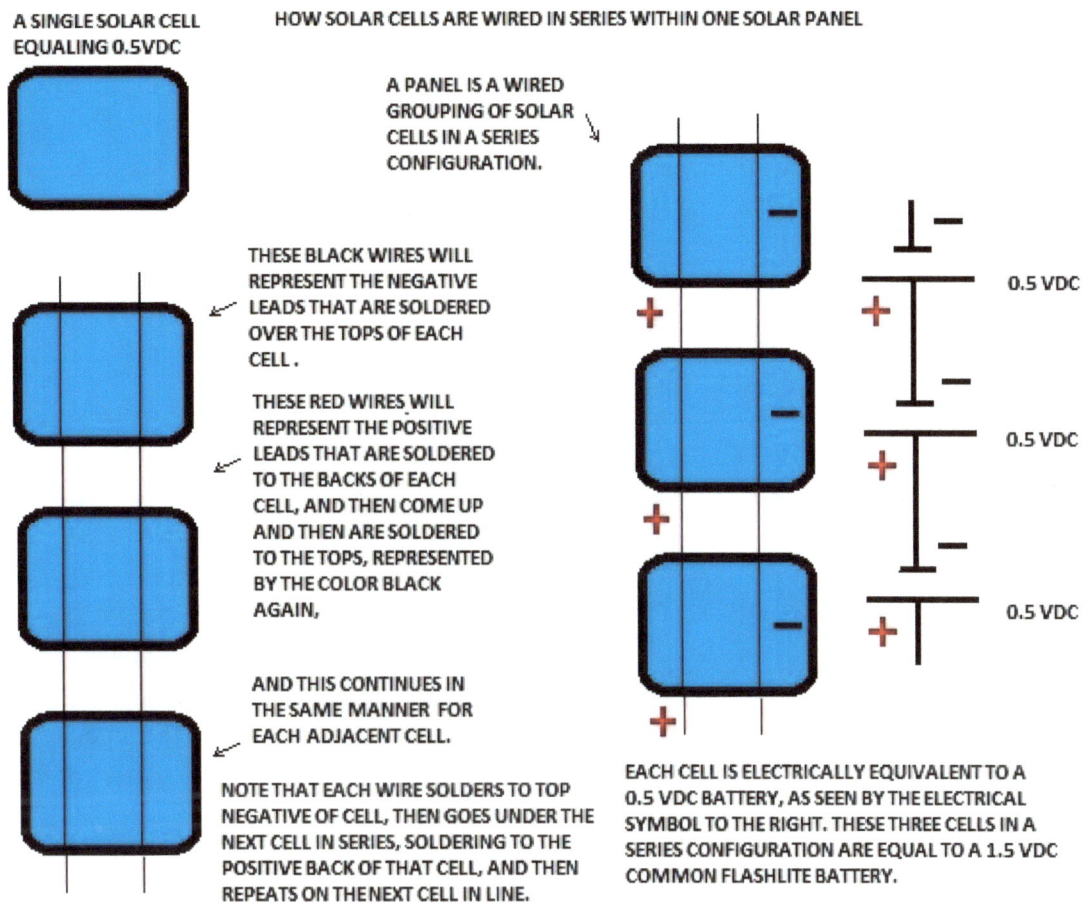

A SINGLE SOLAR CELL EQUALING 0.5VDC

HOW SOLAR CELLS ARE WIRED IN SERIES WITHIN ONE SOLAR PANEL

A PANEL IS A WIRED GROUPING OF SOLAR CELLS IN A SERIES CONFIGURATION.

THESE BLACK WIRES WILL REPRESENT THE NEGATIVE LEADS THAT ARE SOLDERED OVER THE TOPS OF EACH CELL.

THESE RED WIRES WILL REPRESENT THE POSITIVE LEADS THAT ARE SOLDERED TO THE BACKS OF EACH CELL, AND THEN COME UP AND THEN ARE SOLDERED TO THE TOPS, REPRESENTED BY THE COLOR BLACK AGAIN,

AND THIS CONTINUES IN THE SAME MANNER FOR EACH ADJACENT CELL.

NOTE THAT EACH WIRE SOLDERS TO TOP NEGATIVE OF CELL, THEN GOES UNDER THE NEXT CELL IN SERIES, SOLDERING TO THE POSITIVE BACK OF THAT CELL, AND THEN REPEATS ON THE NEXT CELL IN LINE.

0.5 VDC

0.5 VDC

0.5 VDC

EACH CELL IS ELECTRICALLY EQUIVALENT TO A 0.5 VDC BATTERY, AS SEEN BY THE ELECTRICAL SYMBOL TO THE RIGHT. THESE THREE CELLS IN A SERIES CONFIGURATION ARE EQUAL TO A 1.5 VDC COMMON FLASHLITE BATTERY.

Every solar panel begins with a single solar cell. It is wired to a second cell, then a third, and so on until the number of cells are soldered in a series configuration for the total voltage desired. For example, a 12 volt panel requires 36 cells in series, a 24 volt panel requires 60, and a 48 volt panel requires 72.

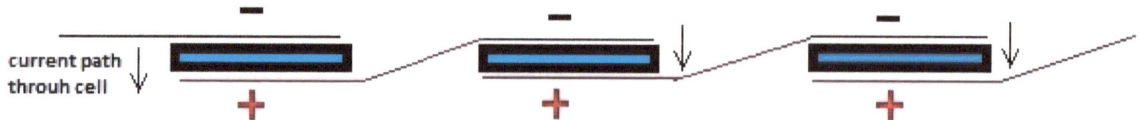

SIDE VIEW OF THREE SOLAR CELLS WITH TABBING WIRES SOLDERED AS SHOWN:

THE NEGATIVE WIRE (REPRESENTED BY COLOR BLACK HERE) IS SOLDERED ATOP THE SOLAR CELL.
THE POSITIVE WIRE (REPRESENTED BY COLOR RED HERE) IS SOLDERED BELOW THE SOLAR CELL.
THIS CONFIGURATION PLACES THE STRING OF CELLS INTO SERIES, EACH VOLTAGE ADDING TO THE NEXT.

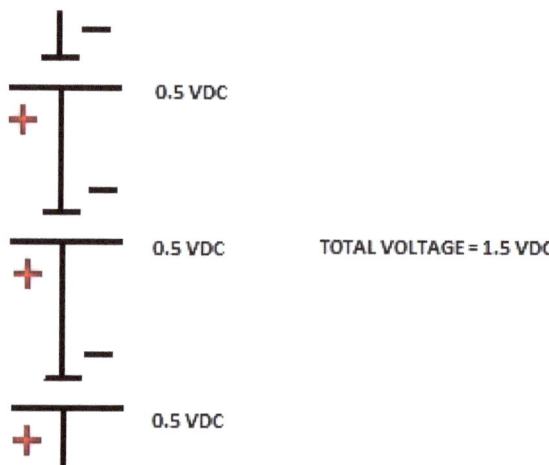

Each cell, when in light, will offer 0.5 volts DC at its output and a current that varies with the amount of light (photons) striking the cell. Stringing cells in series increases the voltage needed for a 12v battery or for a 12v, 24v, or 48v inverter.

Each completed panel has a rear plastic enclosure containing (or should contain) bypass diodes to redirect the current around any cells within the panel that become shaded, so to save the cell from overheating as other cells' active currents would pass through the shaded cell. This would be a serious cause of damage if these diodes were not in place.

The next image is the plastic enclosure located on the back of the solar panel, and it is where the cells' wiring is threaded through and connected (clipped) onto contacts that the AWG 12 cables are attached to.
A plastic cover is pressed down and clipped onto the enclosure, and may be easily removed with a small flat head screwdriver.

The enclosure is fastened to the back with epoxy and when closed up is weather-tight.

There are six bypass diodes installed into the enclosure. Please see TERMINOLOGY section for information. In that same enclosure are the series connection wires, positive and negative, that would pass through weather fittings as a single positive wire and a negative wire. These two wires (usually AWG 12) have MC4 special, weather-tight connectors and could be interconnected with other panels' MC4 connectors into series or parallel configurations to increase either voltage and/or current total output.

These are weather-tight MC4 connectors, two per panel, a positive and a negative.

This wiring would eventually be connected to a DC Fast Breaker/Switch, then to a Charge Controller.
The panel has an aluminum frame around it with a protective glass front against most weather issues.
Panel's weight depends on number of cells. About 12 lbs for 36 cell panel, and about 50 lbs for 60 cells.
There are various other cell configurations for smaller panels too. The above sizes are those usually put into roof and ground mount arrays.

The finished product is tested and a label describing the measured parameters is affixed to the back of the panel, here is a graphical on a type of label seen :

EACH SOLAR PANEL HAS A LABEL ON ITS BACK LISTING SPECIFICATIONS, INCLUDING MAXIMUM RATED POWER, VOLTAGE AND CURRENT. THESE RATED PARAMETERS SHOULD NOT BE EXCEEDED.

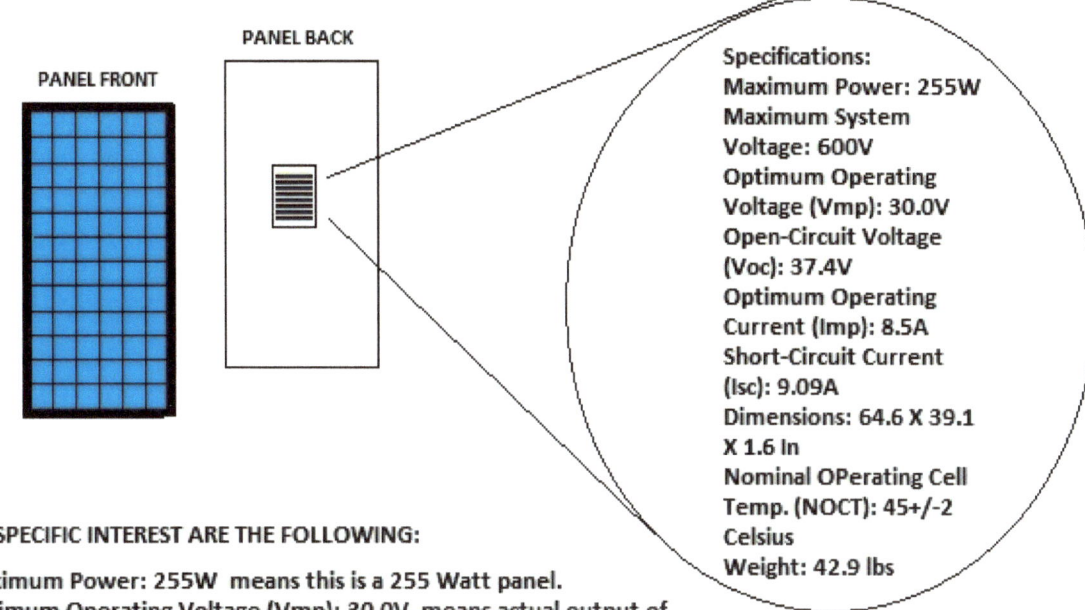

OF SPECIFIC INTEREST ARE THE FOLLOWING:

--Maximum Power: 255W means this is a 255 Watt panel.
--Optimum Operating Voltage (Vmp): 30.0V means actual output of
   this panel is 24 V (The Nominal Voltage)
--Optimum Operating Current (Imp): 8.5A means actual current
   output of this panel is 8 Amps (The Nominal Current)

BATTERIES/INVERTERS

Batteries are an essential part of the off-grid, stand-alone solar power set-up. The two uses of solar batteries are to store the energy delivered to them from the solar panels, and provide energy, as needed, to your home. The energy from batteries is offered directly to your VDC, Voltage Direct Current, devices and appliances and/or to your VAC, Voltage Alternating Current, appliances, etc. via a solar power inverter. Most homes use VAC electrical power. Recreational vehicles tend to use VDC or hook up to VAC depending on availability.

Let's say you wanted to wire a space in your house just for VDC appliances. You could use a bank of 12 volt batteries to supply current to those.

Consider an example:

The room has LED lighting using VDC. It requires 2 amps for the string of lights. You have a 100 AH (Amp Hour) battery. If we do the math, 100 AH divided by 2 amps/hour will equal 50 hours of lighting on 100 amps. That's a lot of free sun power!

Of course, you would not use the full supply from the battery because that can wear down your battery life more quickly. It's usually the practice to discharge a battery to approximately 50% of capacity. 100 amps being the capacity in this example. But, that still gives us 25 hours of free energy between recharges. It's still free lighting for 25 hours.

Now, let's try staying with the common VAC we already have in the house lighting. We utilize the same 100 AH battery to power a 100 watt VAC bulb in that space instead. We still want to use solar. So, we need to add a solar inverter between the battery output and the bulb. An inverter converts the battery's VDC, direct current, into VAC, alternating current, which the bulb wants. An inverter's internal electronics is going to compensate for the need to bring the battery's 12 volts DC up to the needed 120 volts AC for that bulb, the same VAC you have at every outlet in a common house wiring. By so doing, the inverter has to use more current—more amps—to make this work. What steps up, in transformer logic, must step down. An inverter's electronics can step up the 12 VDC input to 120 VAC output only by increasing the Amps taken from the battery to compensate the ratio. You'll notice the ratio of 12 to 120 is 1:10, and that has to be compensated for by taking more amps at a reverse ratio of 10:1 from the battery.

That 100 watt bulb normally needs 0.83 amps to light, under the 120 VAC, but the inverter will require about ten times that current at its input, around ten amps, to do so. Where does it get those ten amps? It comes from the battery. So, that 100 watt bulb that only needed 0.83 amps/hour to work, now needs 10 amps/hour from the battery into the inverter per hour to work. This being due to the inverter having to convert the 12 VDC input to the inverter up to 120 VAC output level to light the bulb.

My solar panels are manufactured as 24 VDC panels, not 12 VDC as in the above example. So, I installed a 24 VDC inverter instead of 12 VDC, bringing about a ratio of 1:5 through the inverter, 24 volts times five equals 120 volts VAC out of the inverter. That's an advantage of going to a 24 VDC setup, rather than 12 VDC setup. I cut the amps draw from the battery bank in half, going to the inverter. Still, using an inverter on a 12 VDC or 24 VDC setup will take more amps from the battery bank than would directly putting VDC into the home by using only DC, Direct Current, appliances instead of the normal VAC appliances. Therefore, the 100 AH battery will discharge much sooner than if using a direct current set of LED lights needing only 2 amps per hour out of the battery.

This is why some folks go to 12 VDC or even 24 VDC appliances in the home, and it is a good transition. It is just the overall cost involved to replace most or all of the VAC appliances. Note too, there are not many 24 VDC lighting fixtures or appliances on the market, yet. 12 VDC is doing better. In starting up a solar set-up, using the inverter is a good start so to keep costs down going full VDC. One day that inverter may come out of the system and direct DC will be king. For now, "mygrid" and "their Grid" works.

My thinking (if you're interested) is, it's free energy from the sun, deep cycle solar batteries last 5 + years, you may add more batteries into the bank to compensate for the increased inverter input amps, and inverters allow use of the same wiring and appliances already in-house.

I can see a mixture of both types of current if you want to try things anyway. I did try a hybrid DC/AC for an 80 gallon hot water tank, which was interesting to do. I put two 24 VDC solar panels in series to obtain 48 VDC output and connected it to the lower heating element in the tank. I did swap out the lower element with a 120 VAC one. The element's resistance was 7 ohms. It is simply a resistor. Putting 48 VDC into it, doing the math, I = V/R, gave me a current (I) of 7 amps. Enough to heat the water, and that 7 amps continues all day the sun is out. I adjusted the element's thermostat to a safe level to compensate. This is one idea for direct DC use. The upper element remained the 240 VAC one that came with the tank, thus making this tank a hybrid configuration. **Note**: I have determined a 40 gallon tank with the single 120VAC element being connected to a VDC source is more practical than 80 gallon hybrid.

Another note: Besides going hybrid on your 80 gallon hot water tank, to save electrical costs, you could put an electrical timer on the tank's power input. You can set the timer to power up the tank heating elements early in the morning and have it shut off later. They usually have six separate timing settings for throughout the day. It does save on that electrical bill!

Batteries do have a shelf life. My personal experience with lead acid batteries is they last 3 years in New England, then fade in starting power strength. You do not want to try getting to work on the 5th year in 5 degrees below zero or worse! That's just my opinion, of course. This type of battery is meant for quick starting of vehicles, etc. and has high "cold cranking amp" ratings. This lead acid is not very useful for solar.

Solar batteries are very well built. I like the AGM, Absorbable Glass Mat, deep cycle type. For a lead acid battery, these are great for multiple charging/discharging cycles. They have thicker plates and are sealed. I have been using them in the "mygrid" set-up.

AH, Amp Hours, is a rating established from testing. It may be useful as a benchmark rating in the purchasing of solar batteries. If I purchase a 100 AH battery, I do not expect to see my 5 amps/hour appliance last me 20 hours, even 10 hours on a 50% charging cycle. However, it is a rating that helps me assess battery performance.

If I want a solar power set-up for 1000 watts, I would consider how many amps per hour is desired for the particular appliances that will be connected into the system. As you can note from the above information on inverters, that amount of amps must be raised up to compensate using an inverter, too. At this instant, 100 AH batteries seem practical. I get 50 amps for 1 hour, 10 amps for 5 hours, etc., duly noting the actual AH versus labeled AH rating.

Experience in solar indicates you can start low and increase more panels, more battery storage, and add a higher capacity inverter into your set-up over time. Starting with a 500 watt, 1000 watt (1Kw) system, then adding components as money allows, for 2 Kw, 3 Kw configurations, allows for increasing voltage and amps as needed, too.

You could call it, "practical solar"?

CONNECTING IT TOGETHER

Photos and drawings help us visualize a completed set-up. Let's walk through putting a 1000 watt, 24 VDC, 32 Amp solar set-up into working order:

1. Install the four 250 watt panels to your desired mounting. I decided on a lean-to mounting, attached to weatherized 2 X 6's and secured to my house corner and a small shed at an angle which captures about six hours of direct sunlight per day.

FIG 1

FIG 2

2. Run all cabling through schedule 40 (light gray) PVC to protect wiring from exposure to light and weather. This photo shows the cabling run from panels into the house, with troubleshooting access.

FIG 3

3. Install the four positive (+)red connector cables into an enclosure (see above), connecting them to
    a rated 45 amp terminal block. The numbers above coincide with each of the four solar panels.
    Then connect individual Schottky blocking diodes to each cable over to a second terminal block.
    At the second terminal block, connect copper jumpers from each of the lower three terminals over
    to its adjacent terminal. Connect wiring from that 2nd block's top terminal (red connector), through
    the enclosure hole to a 40 amp DC Fast Breaking switch (see FIG 6). From the DC Fast Breaker,
    Connect an AWG 12 (AWG 8, if wire length is over 4 feet) to the Charge Controller "Solar" positive (+)
    input (port 1, FIG 7). This becomes a basic combiner box that combines the four positive cables, via
    the terminal blocks, into a single positive wire going to the DC Breaker and eventually to the charge
    controller (+) input.

17

4. Install the four negative (-) cables into the same enclosure, connecting them to another terminal Block (The upper block),indicated by the blue connectors.You would also add copper jumpers to this block's bottom terminals. then connect an AWG 12 (AWG 8) (the single blue connector) through the enclosure hole, directly to the Charge Controller "Solar" negative (-) input (port 2). This action combines the four negative cables of the panels, via a terminal block, into a single negative wire going to the charge controller's negative connection point.

   Note: Having all panels' cabling meeting in an enclosure makes a good troubleshooting step. You could easily test each panel's voltage using a multi-meter.

5. **Optional**: May want to connect a DC Digital Multi-function Meter between the charge controller and the battery bank, to have a visual of volts, amps, and power going into the batteries. This is a very useful device also for troubleshooting. The meter includes a 100 amp shunt.

FIG 4

FIG 5

100 Amp Shunts. Top one works with first meter above between charge controller and battery bank. Bottom shunt works between battery bank and the inverter.

FIG 4 shows the two multi-meters' LCDs installed through cutouts in the black plastic 4X5 file box. Their respective 100 amp shunts were placed inside the box, onto its bottom. I used two pieces of paint stiring sticks to fasten the shunts to, and made all connections per a very good diagram that comes with these meters and shunts. Take your time and you'll have no problem. Looking at FIG 4, You'll see the **26.15 v** on both meters indicates the battery's actual measured voltage (at the time of my taking this photo). Full charge on the batteries is about 28-29 volts. The **3.48 A** is the measured current, in amps, the Charge Controller is putting into the battery bank, from the solar panels. Depending on time of day and amount of sunlight, this setup has gone up to about 32 amps on a bright sunny day. The **0.00 A** on the left meter indicates the current, in amps, being drawn from the battery bank to the inverter. I had the inverter off at this time. You can see the value of these meters. You can monitor volts, amps, and power from panels to battery bank, and to inverter easily. It is an excellent visual in your setup!

FIG 6

This is the DC Fast Breaker/Switch, rated 40 Amps, that the single red positive wire will pass through , from the combiner, before going to the charge controller. Notice there is space for additional DC Breakers. The cover slides forward to insert other breakers by sliding them onto rails.

Additional breakers, of varying amperage, may be inserted so to supply VDC directly to DC operated devices. Usually, a Fast Breaker or more is added after the battery bank, going into separate inverters too. That is a bit more down the road as money and needs occur.

6. Run AWG 4 (battery cables) from the charge controller's positive and negative battery output ports, over to the battery bank configured for 24 VDC: The 12 volt batteries are configured into two batteries in series, giving 24 volts output at half the rated amperage. Later, you could purchase two additional 12 volt batteries for more power.

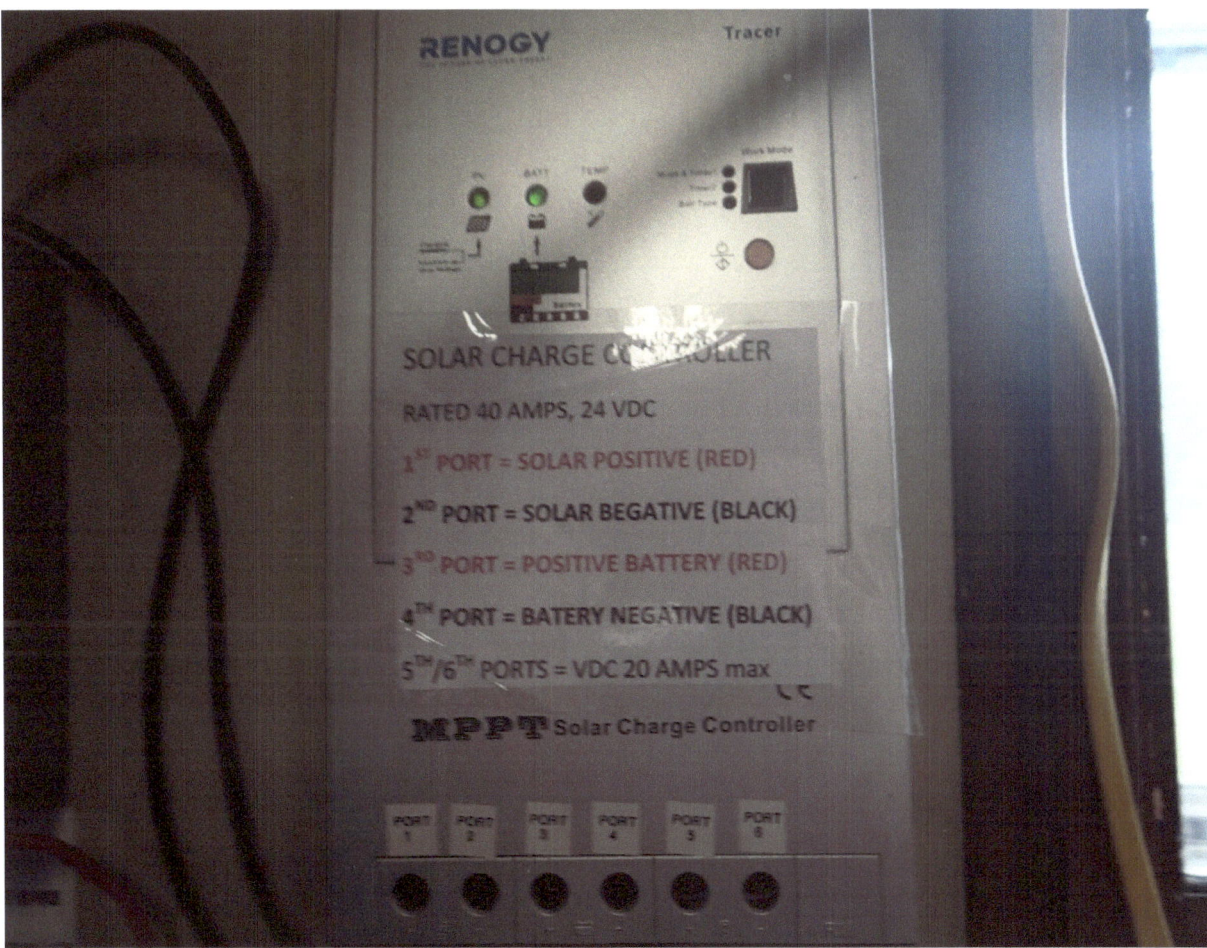

FIG 7

This is an MPPT, Multi-Power Point Tracking, Charge Controller

First green LED indicates solar panels seeing photon energy. Second LED indicates battery bank is charging.

At full charge the LED will start flashing. Third LED is a temperature sensor.

FIG 8

Two 100 AH Deep Cycle Batteries, connected two 12 volt in series for 24 VDC, 100 Amp output

FIG 9

7. Run AWG 4 cables to the inverter's input connections. Red to positive, black to negative from the batteries' output connections. This view is of the front end of the inverter.

8. **Optional**: May also connect a 2nd DC Digital Multi-function Meter between the battery bank output, and the inverter input. This meter also includes a 100 amp shunt (see item 5 above).

FIG 10

You plug a 120 VAC appliance into the back two outlets

LIGHTNING

A bolt of lightning is six times hotter than the sun (9980 degrees) at 54,000 degrees! Lightning seeks paths of low impedance. Air offers more impedance to a bolt than does a tree or other object. The bolt of lightning would take the path through the tree and not try going through the air next to it.

It seeks pointy objects such as a lightning rod on top of a barn, a tree top, a spire atop a building, you standing in a field. Pointy things tend to have a larger buildup of positive charges on them, which attracts the negatively charged energy in the bolt.

It will seek high objects such as trees and tall buildings, but if those are not present, then anything will do. It will strike the sap in a tree causing it to explode, cracking it.

Five miles up, a cloud develops a charged electron (negative) grouping which causes energy lines to spread out at various angles. These lines of energy then spread further outwards as negatively charged particles move toward the earth.

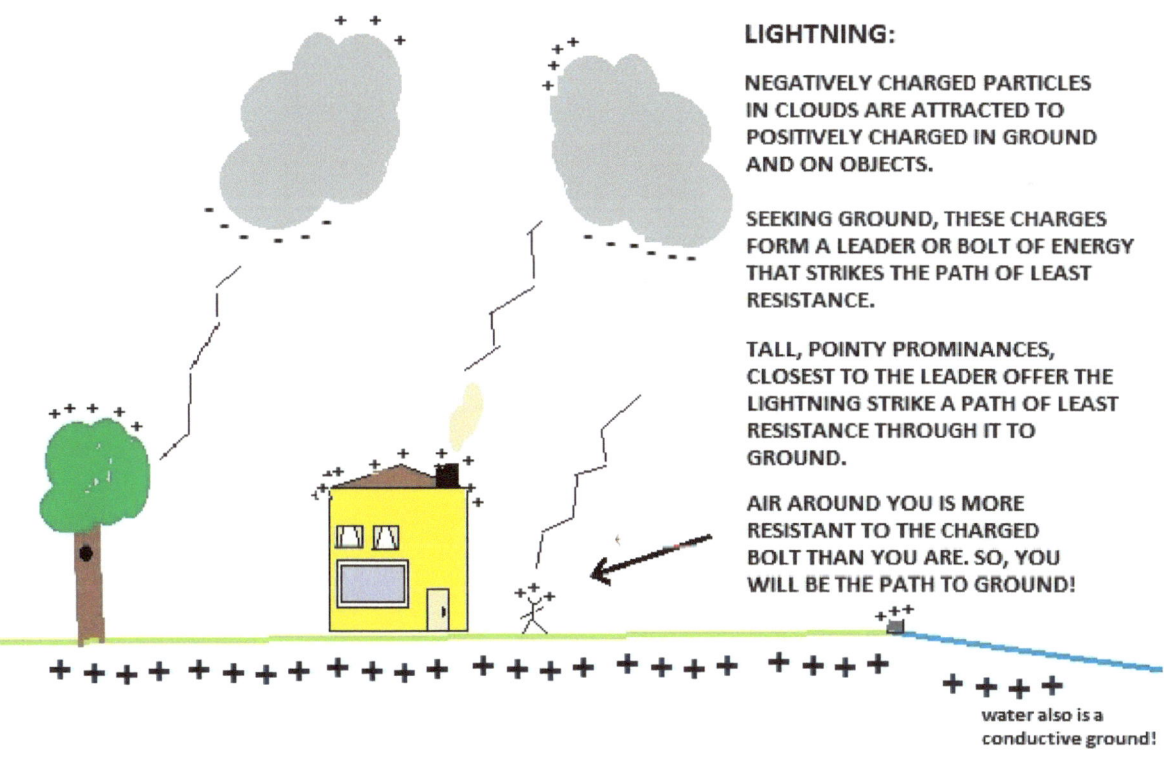

LIGHTNING:

NEGATIVELY CHARGED PARTICLES IN CLOUDS ARE ATTRACTED TO POSITIVELY CHARGED IN GROUND AND ON OBJECTS.

SEEKING GROUND, THESE CHARGES FORM A LEADER OR BOLT OF ENERGY THAT STRIKES THE PATH OF LEAST RESISTANCE.

TALL, POINTY PROMINANCES, CLOSEST TO THE LEADER OFFER THE LIGHTNING STRIKE A PATH OF LEAST RESISTANCE THROUGH IT TO GROUND.

AIR AROUND YOU IS MORE RESISTANT TO THE CHARGED BOLT THAN YOU ARE. SO, YOU WILL BE THE PATH TO GROUND!

water also is a conductive ground!

At earth level, the positive ions will form lines that lift upwards to possibly meet with these negative charges coming down, thus making a connection. Then a high energy and frequency burst of some 10,000 amperes of current flows in that strike we call lightning. The natural static build-up on objects and the ground can be in the path of that energy.

A solar panel also is statically charged and can receive a strike too, which can destroy it or at least the bypass diodes and some conductor paths.

To try protecting the panel, an AWG 6 solid (or stranded, easier to work with and skin effect better) copper wire is connected to each panels' aluminum frame at multiple points, and then to an 8 foot solid copper rod. This rod is hammered into the earth to most of its length, with a clamp fastener (or two) tightened against the rod's exposed, top portion.

The above image shows a lug that is bolted or screwed into a solar panel's aluminum frame. These are placed about a foot apart down each frame on one side, then the AWG 6 copper is tightly fastened as seen using the screw-down. In NEC terms, the copper cable is called a "GEC", Grounding Electrode Conductor. The eight foot copper rod hammered into the ground is simply called an "electrode". The cable is attached tightly to the rod with one or two grounding clamps, as shown below.

The NEC, National Electrical Code, calls these rods "electrodes", and more than one may be installed to

 improve protection.

For the type of grounding cable to use, see NEC code:250.62 Grounding Electrode Conductor Material. The grounding electrode conductor shall be of copper, aluminum, or copper-clad aluminum. The material selected shall be resistant to any corrosive condition existing at the installation or shall be protected against corrosion. The conductor shall be solid or stranded, insulated, covered, or bare.

Electronics includes math problems = cannot escape it - but they are simplified below. It is basically working with Ohms law, which can help you better understand what is going on in the various components of a complete operating solar set-up. Measurements are taken with a meter, then you can assess what might happen, what power you could obtain, by working the math out, and these following few equations will help you do that on paper, before you make changes to the set-up.

SOLAR MATH

The following formulas are useful in calculating a specific value, where one of the three is missing:

Solar Panel Current output is calculated by dividing the power (in watts) by the Voltage (in volts), using the formula:

$$I = \frac{P}{V}$$

P	**Power (in Watts)**
I	**Current (in Amps)**
V	**Voltage (in Volts)**

Solar Panel Power output is calculated by multiplying the Current (in amps) by the Voltage:

$$P = I * V$$

Solar Panel Voltage is calculated by dividing the Power by the Current:

$$V = \frac{P}{I}$$

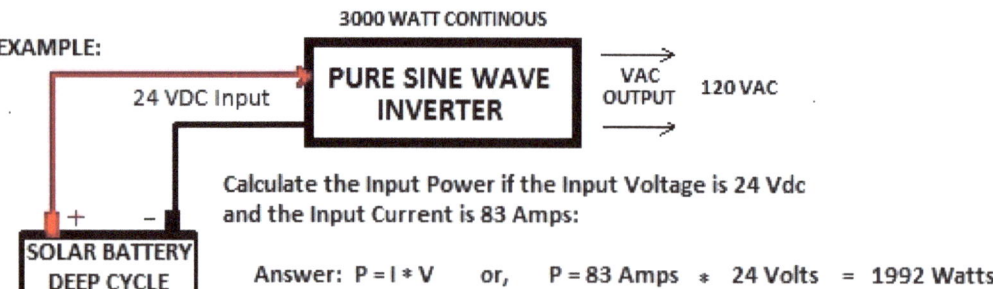

EXAMPLE:

3000 WATT CONTINOUS

24 VDC Input | **PURE SINE WAVE INVERTER** | VAC OUTPUT | 120 VAC

SOLAR BATTERY DEEP CYCLE

Calculate the Input Power if the Input Voltage is 24 Vdc and the Input Current is 83 Amps:

Answer: P = I * V   or,   P = 83 Amps * 24 Volts = 1992 Watts

INVERTERS TRANSFORM A DC INPUT VOLTAGE INTO EITHER A 120 OR 240 (OR BOTH) OUTPUT AC VOLTAGE.

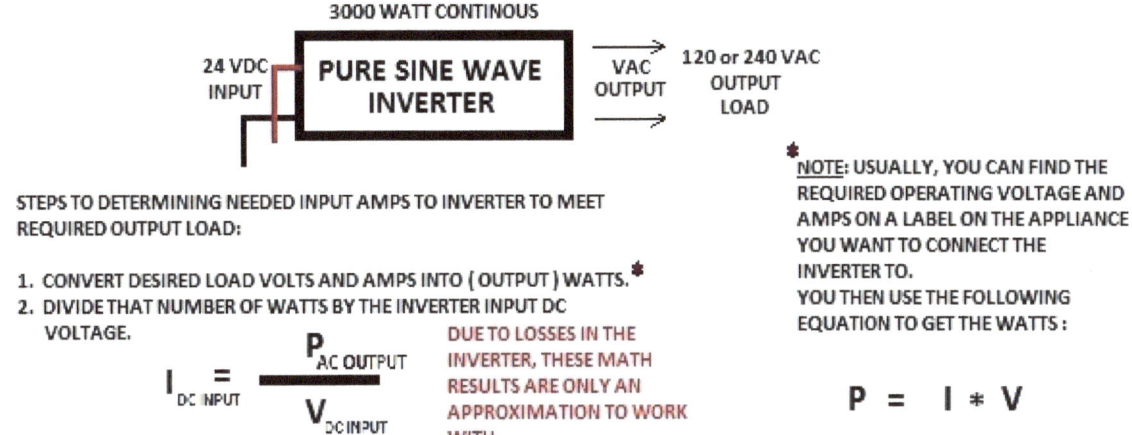

STEPS TO DETERMINING NEEDED INPUT AMPS TO INVERTER TO MEET REQUIRED OUTPUT LOAD:

1. CONVERT DESIRED LOAD VOLTS AND AMPS INTO (OUTPUT) WATTS. *
2. DIVIDE THAT NUMBER OF WATTS BY THE INVERTER INPUT DC VOLTAGE.

$$I_{DC\ INPUT} = \frac{P_{AC\ OUTPUT}}{V_{DC\ INPUT}}$$

DUE TO LOSSES IN THE INVERTER, THESE MATH RESULTS ARE ONLY AN APPROXIMATION TO WORK WITH.

* NOTE: USUALLY, YOU CAN FIND THE REQUIRED OPERATING VOLTAGE AND AMPS ON A LABEL ON THE APPLIANCE YOU WANT TO CONNECT THE INVERTER TO.
YOU THEN USE THE FOLLOWING EQUATION TO GET THE WATTS :

$$P = I * V$$

EXAMPLE: WANT TO POWER A 1/2 HP, 240 VAC 1.5 AMP DEEP WELL PUMP?

FIRST NEED TO CONVERT HP (HORSEPOWER) TO ELECTRICAL WATTS.
PUMP WATTS = (1/2 HP) * (746 WATTS/HP) = 373 WATTS

THEN, DIVIDE THE NUMBER OF WATTS BY INVERTER INPUT DC VOLTS OF 24 VDC, EQUALS 15.5 AMPS.   THEREFORE, NEED 15.5 AMPS OUT OF BATTERY BANK GOING INTO INVERTER TO SUPPLY OUTPUT OF 240 VAC. 1.5 AMP TO THE PUMP.

REMEMBER, SOME APPLIANCES HAVE A START UP CURRENT. THE ABOVE EXAMPLE OF 15.5 AMPS IS THE CONTINUOUS CURRENT NEED AFTER AN INITIAL PUMP MOTOR STARTS UP. THAT IS WHY INVERTERS ARE LABELED CONTINUOUS POWER/SURGE POWER.

Multi-meters measure watts, amps, and volts. Math offers paperwork changes ahead of component reworking. Hand-in-hand, it works out the kinks: a good process.

Resistance in solar circuits and its wiring need a mathematic consideration too.

This is the electronic symbol for a Resistor

This resistor has the element Carbon in it. When current passes through it, some of the electrons' energy is dissipated into the carbon as heat energy. The electronics world uses resistors in circuits to drop out some of the voltage not needed by a "Load", for example, a 6 volt, 0.5 amp rated bulb

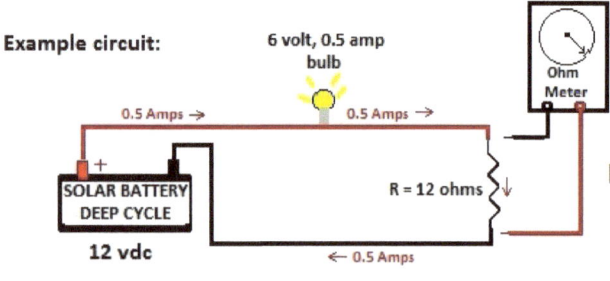

Example circuit:

6 volt, 0.5 amp bulb

Ohm Meter

0.5 Amps →   0.5 Amps →

+
SOLAR BATTERY
DEEP CYCLE

R = 12 ohms

12 vdc   ← 0.5 Amps

$$R = \frac{6\ volts}{0.5\ amps} = 12\ ohms$$

Thus, the required current for the bulb can be controlled by adding a resistor into the circuit to drop the unused volts as well as set the amperage level to avoid a blown out bulb due to much higher amp flow through it

The bulb requires 6 volts and 0.5 amps to make it light.

Its voltage source is a 12 volt battery.

We can ensure the bulb only gets 0.5 amps by using a resistor to drop out the remaining 6 volts,

12 v battery - 6 volts bulb = 6 volts left.

Here is the math to find how much resistance is needed to have only 0.5 amps flowing in the circuit:

$$R = \frac{V}{I}$$

AWG, American Wire Gauge, also controls how much amperage a wire is allowed to pass through it, just as the circuit controls its current for the particular load. The solar panel may provide about 8 amps output in bright sun light. The AWG chart would indicate using an AWG 12 wire on the panel. Most panels come with 12 gauge wiring. Remember that wiring has resistance and the longer the length used the more heat loss. It is a good practice to utilize AWG charts to determine what size wiring to use depending on current flow and distance between your panels and the solar electronics on your setup.

FULL PARTS LIST

(4) 250 watt, 24 VDC Solar Panels, with MC4, AWG 12 cables connected

(1) MPPT Solar Charge Controller, 24 VDC, 40 Amps

(2) "DC digital multi-function meter", Product Model PZEM-051. An excellent meter and shunt,

  with instructions. Can find on Amazon.

(1) Plastic ABS NEMA box w/latching solid door, approx measurements: 8" X 6" X 4"

(3) Dual Row 4 Position Screw Terminal Block, rated 45 Amps, 600 Volts

(10) Insulated Fork Spade Wire Connector Crimp Terminal, AWG 12/10

(4) Schottky Blocking Diode, rated 15 Amps

(20) Amphenol Industrial HGLU-10 Helio Lug, Bolt-On Coupling, AWG 4, Screw termination

(10) 3/8 Tinned Copper Lug Terminal, AWG 4 (goes onto battery cable ends, use with TEMCO Hammer Lug Crimper Tool)

(1) 24 Volt 3000 Watt Peak/6000 Watt Surge Pure Sine Wave Inverter

(2) AGM Deep Cycle 100 Amp Hour 12 volt Battery for PV Solar (larger sizes AmpHour optional)

(1) 25 feet Battery OFC, Black, AWG 4, 25 feet Battery OFC Cable, Red, AWG 4

(1) Copper Grounding Rod, 8 feet

(2) Copper Grounding Rod Clamp

(1) 25 feet either solid or stranded AWG 6 copper cable

(1) Solar DC Fast breaker, 40 Amp, 150 VDC

(1) A plastic box with top, hinged cover for the shunted meters (optional). I used a simple black 4 X 5

index card box from Walmart. You cut the front for two meters' LCD screens to fit through.

SPECIAL TOOLS

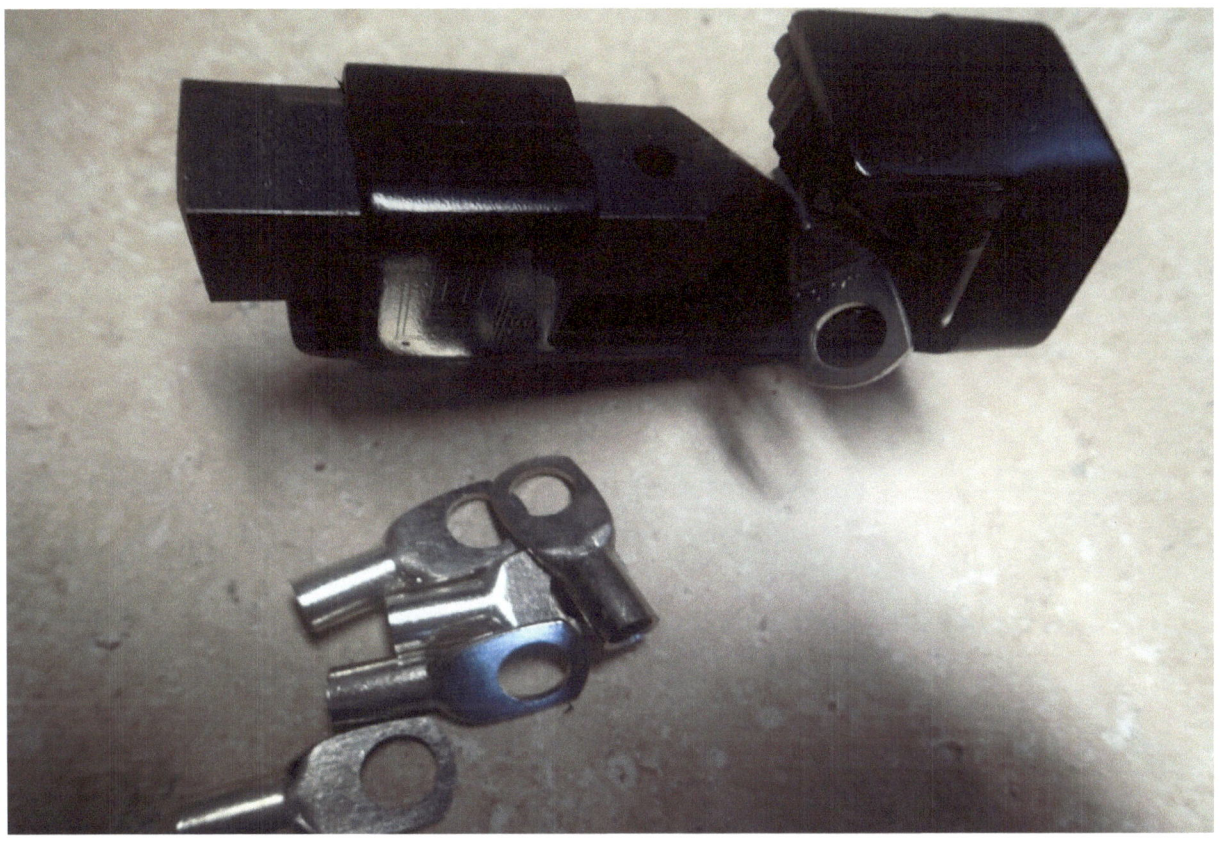

TEMCO Hammer Lug Crimper Tool (for crimping down the battery cable connector, very helpful)

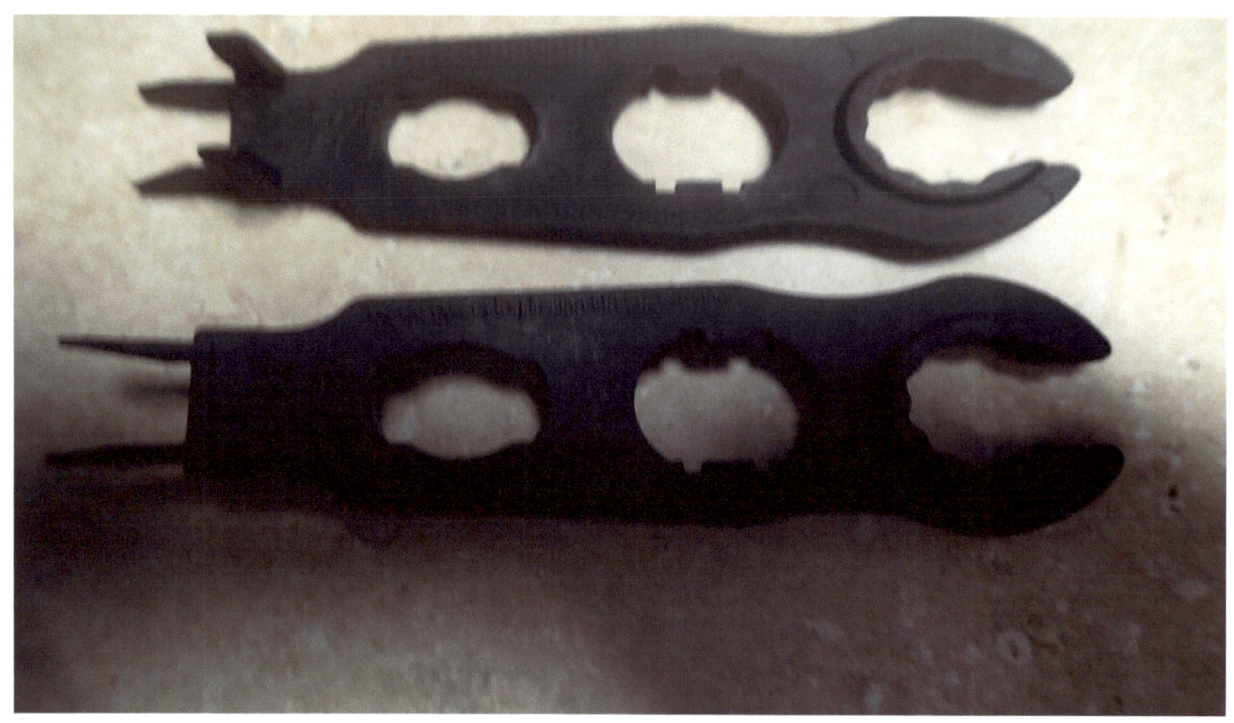

MC4 Solar Panel Assembly Tool, (for assembly/disassembly of MC4 connectors)

Note: There is a complete kit for solar panel MC4 connectors which includes the single connectors, two MC4 tools, a crimping tool, cutter, and a zippered pouch.

Note: Depending on distance between Solar panels and Charger Controller, may need some Solar Panel Extension Cables with MC4 Connectors both ends, AWG 4, 600VDC

A Multi-meter is very needed for testing cabling and inputs/outputs, and troubleshooting.

An inductive amp meter comes in handy too. I use it on the inverter output hot wire for checking amps drawn by different appliances. Just wrap it around the black wire of a power strip I plug each appliance into and plug the strip into the inverter.

TERMINOLOGY

Amp-hour, AH: This term of measurement helps us know how many hours a fully-charged battery may last. Knowing this, we can calculate how many batteries of a certain amp-hour size we need in our particular solar setup's battery bank. For example, to run specific appliances you would require a total of 35 amps per hour out of the battery bank. We have to prevent each battery discharging below 50%, as a rule, so that requires doubling the 35 amps to 70 amps. Now, if through the sunny days there are enough amps providing power to run the appliances as well as charge the battery bank for overnight needs, we can determine the desired battery bank amp-hours. A 70 AH battery size means one battery lasting one hour of continued use, if not noting the 50% discharging limit. So, if we wanted to run appliances all night (i.e., no sunlight), it may require having possibly 10 hours of charge available, or 700 amps stored in that bank. That would be 10 batteries needed. But, we could buy larger AH size batteries to reduce that number. We could use 4 batteries that provide 200 AH storage capacity each. There are various sizes available, just have to pay more of course. Remember, the 70 AH rating on a battery , if we ignore the 50% discharge rule, means there is enough stored power for either 70 amps for one hour, 10 amps for 7 hours, or 7 amps for 10 hours, even 1 amp for 70 hours! It is simply multiplication.

HOW TO DEFINE AH, AMP-HOUR, AND HOW SERIES AND PARALLEL BATTERIES ARE CONFIGURED

EXAMPLE

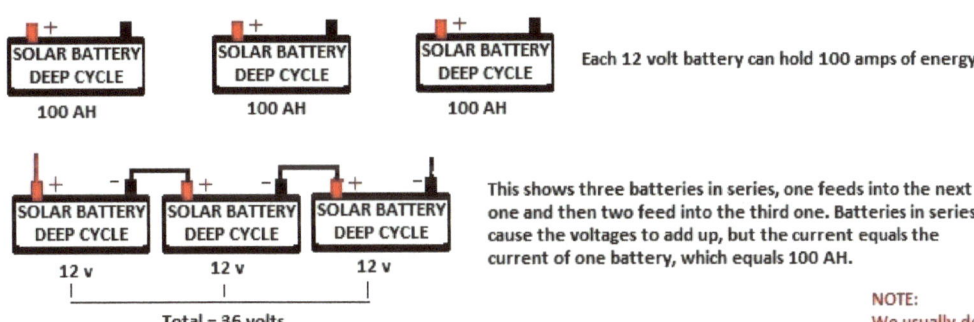

Each 12 volt battery can hold 100 amps of energy.

This shows three batteries in series, one feeds into the next one and then two feed into the third one. Batteries in series cause the voltages to add up, but the current equals the current of one battery, which equals 100 AH.

Total = 36 volts
100 AH

One AH or Amp-hour means a 100 amp-hour battery will last 1 hour on a 100 amp appliance.
If you connected to an appliance needing 10 amps, the 100 AH battery will last 10 hours.
If you connected to an appliance needing 25 amps, the 100 AH battery would last 4 hours.
In a series configuration of batteries, it does not matter how many 12 volt batteries you connect up. The current, called Amps, will still only be 100 amps of energy.

NOTE:
We usually do not let a battery discharge below 50 % of its AH capacity before recharging it. This would wear down the battery sooner, limiting number of recharging cycles in its life time.

So, if you have a 100 AH battery, that would mean only allowing 50 amps drained before each recharging occurs.

There are different AH capacities available. This 100 AH is just one example.

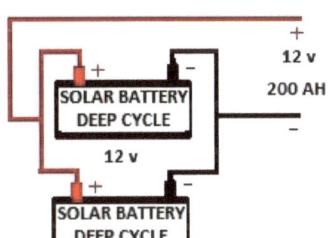

12 v
200 AH

Two batteries in parallel will only equal the voltage of one, 12 volts. But, their current capacity will actually add together, that is, each 100 amps now totals 200 amps. These two 100 AH batteries now provide 200 AH total at 12 volts total.
Now, a 12 volt appliance will have 200 amps for a time dictated by how many amps it requires to operate over how long it needs to within the 200 amp-hour limitation.
If the appliance needs 5 amps, for example, it can run for 200 divided by 5 = 40 hours.

Battery cable: Typical auto battery cables, these are AWG 4 gauge which handle around 250 amps at short lengths of four feet, less amperage as lengths are increased. They come in spools of color black and red, suitable for solar battery banks.

Blocking Diode: This component is usually incorporated into a good solar charge controller or installed between the solar panels and charge controller if necessary. They can be in a combiner box where all the panels' cabling comes in. Its function is to restrict the flow of stored energy (amps) in the battery bank from returning back into the solar panels, usually at night, when the panels are not receiving energy from the sun. The diode allows current flow toward the charge controller/batteries but not back into the panels. Because a diode has a voltage drop of about 0.7 vdc, which does subtract from the vdc reaching the charge controller, it's better to use a Schottky diode for blocking diodes as these have only a 0.4 vdc drop across them.
(See image below.)

Bonding: This is an NEC term regarding system and equipment bonds to ensure safety in faults occurring in either, and attempts to prevent shock and/or damage. Electrons always seek their source, where they were, they tend to return. If they hit a damaged wire in-line, they find another route possibly via added grounding cable, but absent of that, they will take a route through any metal or human contact point back to their voltage source. Equipment components have to be bonded (metal connection) to each other in case there is a fault -damage in one or more of the components. This bonding provides an alternate path back to the voltage source for the electrons.

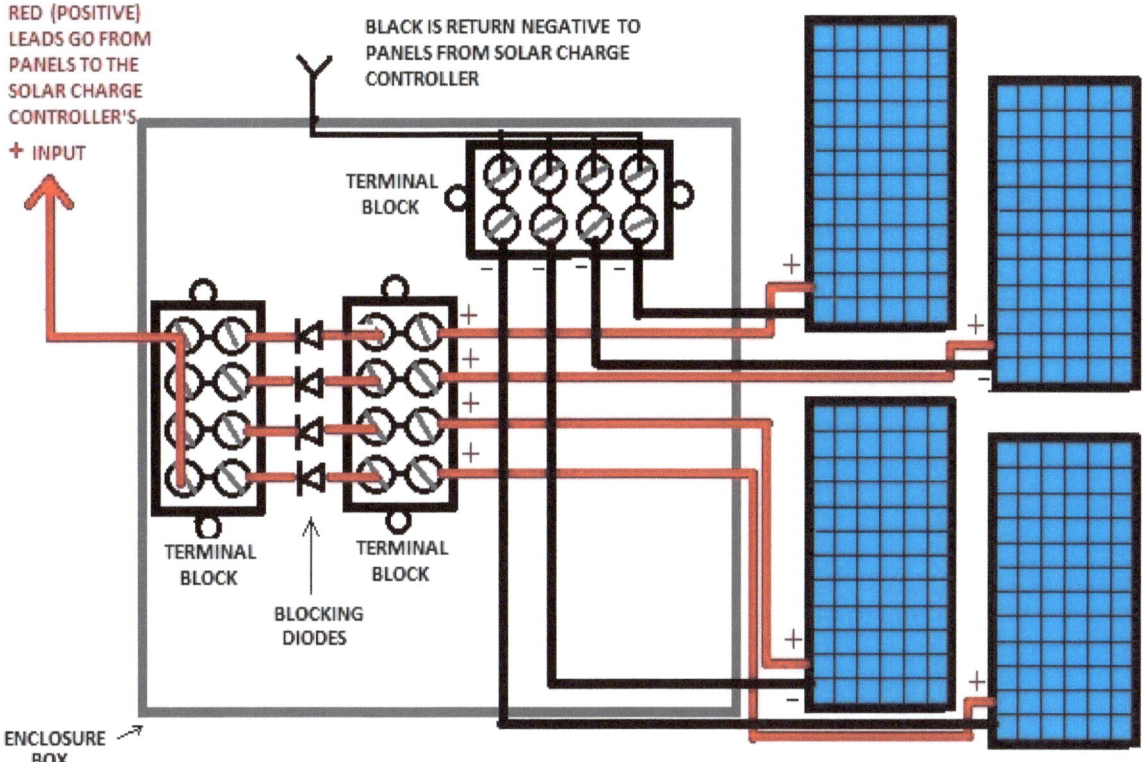

RED (POSITIVE) LEADS GO FROM PANELS TO THE SOLAR CHARGE CONTROLLER'S

+ INPUT

BLACK IS RETURN NEGATIVE TO PANELS FROM SOLAR CHARGE CONTROLLER

TERMINAL BLOCK

TERMINAL BLOCK

TERMINAL BLOCK

BLOCKING DIODES

ENCLOSURE BOX

THE FOUR PANELS ARE CONNECTED IN A PARALLEL CONFIGURATION VIA THESE TERMINAL BLOCKS, INSIDE A WEATHER TIGHT OUTDOOR PLASTIC ENCLOSURE. EACH POSITIVE LEAD (AWG 12) IS SCREWED DOWN ON ONE SIDE OF THE BLOCK, THEN ALL CONNECTIONS ARE JOINED ON THE OUTPUT SIDE OF THE BLOCK INTO ONE SINGLE LEAD (AWG 8) ENDING AT THE SOLAR CHARGE CONTROLLER'S POSITIVE INPUT TERMINAL. BLOCKING DIODES ARE CONNECTED ONLY BETWEEN EACH RED LEAD.

Bypass diode: These diodes are usually installed within the plastic enclosure at the back of a solar panel. Their purpose is to reroute current around each cell which becomes subject to shading, such as from a nearby tree or other object in the path of photons (light) reaching the cell(s). If a cell is shaded, it can heat up due to being in a series configuration that allows other cells to continue moving their charge carriers through, thus heating up and possibly damaging those shaded cells. A good panel will include these bypass diodes.

Charge carriers: Nothing happens without energy being carried or moved through wires and contact points in electronics. Electrons are boosted out of their atoms' orbiting rings and into the conduction band by, in the solar field, photons from the light that produces them. This causes electrons, alias "charge carriers", to basically transport the energy to a load that uses the energy.

Deep cycle battery: Batteries are storage devices. They usually contain metal plates, thin or thick, and an electrolyte catalyst (i.e., sulfuric acid) to create a storage medium of energy for later use. The common lead acid car battery is meant for quick starting bursts of energy (thin plates) and fewer charging cycles in its lifetime. Lead acid solar batteries are deep cycle charging (thick plates) for many cycles, common to solar needs. AGM (Absorbed Glass Mat) are a popular deep cycle solar battery in use today. AH, Amp Hour, is a general rating looked for when considering solar batteries for desired energy capacity needs.

Equipment grounding electrode (EGC): In solar equipment, these are bare, covered, or insulated wiring bonded to all metal enclosures housing electrical/electronic components and wiring. This is normally not carrying current until a fault occurs. Anything with a current flow or may have contact with current flow from faults in other equipment, even in a separate building, would be bonded. Electrons want to return to their source and will use other paths if available. The EGC is purposely installed to control that alternate path so to encourage a breaker to trip and cut off the flow of current stat before it could harm more equipment or persons. Solar charge controller, inverter, meters, aluminum frames will be utilized as a return to source by a fault current. Bonding these together with the EGC hopefully will trip the source breaker and end the flow.

Frame bracket: This aluminum bracket comes in a kit of four with eight 1½ " self-threading brass sheet metal screws for fastening one solar panel to a roof mount. You can change out the screws and install the panel wherever you desire. These brackets are excellent as they slide onto the back aluminum edge of the frame, and you can bolt them onto the frame. Then, you fasten the whole unit to wall, etc by screwing through predrilled holes in the bracket. Here is an image of an installed bracket:

Grounding electrode conductor (GEC): This would be the solid (or stranded) AWG 6 copper cable that gets bonded to the solar panel frame, using the tinned copper lugs. This cable is then bonded (fastened using a copper clamp) to the eight foot solid copper rod, called the "Electrode" per NEC 250.

Grid-tie system: A solar array can be a stand-alone setup, which does not connect into the grid power of a home or industrial site, but if it does, the array's panels may be directly connected to a grid-tie inverter at each panel, or tied into the grid via one larger inverter, then possibly into a transfer switch to dedicated breakers or simply directly into the grid power access with safety shutoffs to prevent shock hazard to electrical line workers. Tying into a power company's grid is under strict observance of codes.

Grounding rod: Usually is an eight-foot-long solid copper rod, having an impedance of less than 25 ohms, that can be hammered into the ground, close to the outside solar array panels. A length of solid or stranded copper cable is connected at intervals along the aluminum frame of each solar panel, then attached finally to the rod(s) using one or more copper clamps. Note: The aluminum frame has an anodized or oxide coating that must be penetrated to make a good conduction contact point for individual lugs that would bolt to the frame and hold the copper grounding cable secure. Usually, drilling through the frame would cut through this coating for a good contact.

Inverter: This device converts Voltage Direct Current, VDC, into Voltage Alternating Current, VAC, for use in solar setups, to supply common AC voltages found in residential/commercial uses. Solar panels provide direct current, but most homes use alternating current. The better inverter is a "Pure Sine Wave Inverter". It utilizes electronic switching components to resemble the AC sine wave form common to household VAC that appliances can work with. "A Modified Sine Wave Inverter" is another, less expensive inverter that can closely resemble the desired sine wave but some appliances may not operate well, such as motors and lighting.

Load: When power is applied to an appliance, for example a fan, that fan is considered as drawing current and therefore, is drawing a load. Thus, the appliance is labeled as a load in the solar electronics field.

MPPT: Multi-Power Point Tracking, MPPT, is an algorithm programmed into a Solar Charge Controller device so to sample the Vmp, nominal voltage, out of the solar array at intervals. If more Vmp is measured than is needed for the required, stable, battery charging voltage, those extra charge carriers of current are sent to the battery bank, thus adding more amps to storage. Remember that solar power in watts equals the Voltage times the current. If the charge controller sees more voltage than is needed to charge the battery, it basically takes that extra voltage and utilizes it as additional charge carriers of energy going into storage for use as needed in a load. It is a great way to increase efficiency.

Photon: There is no solar without the photon! Energy from sunlight is what this particle brings to earth. Because the photon has energy and a frequency component, it is actually a particle of energy and a wave, but it is not an electron. Energy possessed by a moving electron will be dissipated as the electron seeks equilibrium or its rest state. This dissipated burst of energy emitted by the electron is called a quanta; sometimes also referred to as a photon. Yes, a photon comes from light, but it can also be given off, or scattered by an energized electron. A photon travels at light speed (in a vacuum). There is a constant that is calculated to represent a quantum of energy over a period of time.

One quantum is **hf**, "h" being Planck's Constant, "f" being the frequency of the particle of radiation, or photon. h = 6.63 E-34 joule-seconds. Then, the kinetic energy of the moving photon is equal to:
KE = h f

Resistor: Also from the Periodic Table of Elements is the element Carbon. Carbon is used in making a very important electronic component called a resistor. The essential property of carbon is in absorbing energy as heat. From the graphical on how electrons carry charge, energy, to appliances in your home, they may need to drop some of that energy due to not being needed to operate the appliance. This energy has to be dissipated, so we insert a resistance to that amount of power, thus causing some of the current to be lost as heat in the carbon. You might touch a resistor and feel the heat of the dropped energy inside the resistor. Wires also possess a small resistance in their copper. This is why it is important to determine how much length of wire we will need to run from solar panels to the solar equipment. The longer the length, the higher the accumulative resistance facing the applied voltage. In our Solar Math graphic on resistance, you can see math is involved in how much current, charge carrying electrons, can actually heat up a wire, thus burning through it. AWG, American Wire Gauge, is a rating given to maximum current (Amperes) that can safely move in certain size wiring and its needed length.

You can find AWG charts online describing which gauge wire is necessary for a particular current and length of wire being used.

Shunt: Meters may require bypassing higher currents around its measuring electronics to prevent damaging the instrument. A simple flat metal, high AWG gauge device is used to shunt most of the current, but still allow the instrument to measure a sample of it, calculating the full current to display onto the meter.

Solar cell: This is the actual component, within the completed solar panel, that receives the sun's energy, as photons, into its doped, silicon substrate. Other elements, such as phosphorous and boron, will be chemically added to the substrate to either add or remove an electron from their atoms' orbits. This develops a semi - conductive medium for the striking photons' energy to displace the electrons into a conduction band and thus into power use or storage. Solar panels consist of a multiple of these cells arranged into a series configuration such as 36 cells in series or 72 cells, to form a direct current voltage. Each cell offers 0.5 VDC. So, 36 cells offer a nominal voltage of 12 VDC output, 60 or 72 cells offer the same 24 VDC output. Cell and Module are not interchangeable terms. A module consists of multiple cells.

Solar Photovoltaic DC Fast Breaker/Switch: NEC (National Electrical Code) requires a fast breaking DC Voltage breaker be used on the input and output of a Charge Controller for protection. The basic AC voltage Breakers found inside residential/commercial AC panels have a delay built-in so to allow seconds before breaking the circuit. This allows for power tools and motors having a surge current need. A solar setup needs to be disconnected instantly to protect its components. This DC Fast Breaker satisfies that need, and is a switch as well.

NOTES:

_____

_____

_____

_____

_____

_____

_____

_____

_____

_____

_____

_____

_____

_____

_____

_____

_____

_____